I0796518

To my three kids and anyone brave enough to rewrite the rules. And above all, to Kathleen, for paving the way. —D.Z.

For all of those who dare to try —J.B.

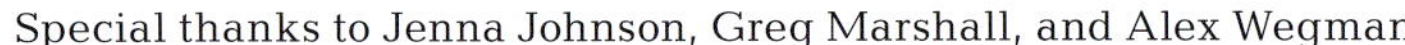

Special thanks to Jenna Johnson, Greg Marshall, and Alex Wegman

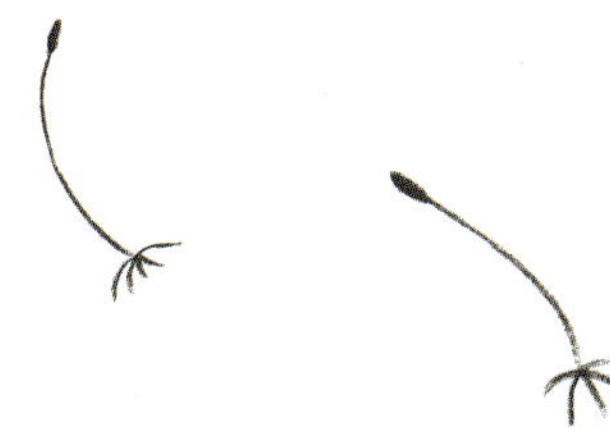

Millbrook Press™
An imprint of Lerner Publishing Group, Inc.
241 First Avenue North
Minneapolis, MN 55401 USA

For reading levels and more information, look up this title at www.lernerbooks.com.

Additional images: courtesy of the author, p. 30; courtesy of Kevin Friel, p. 31; Blueastro/Getty Images, p. 32.

Designed by Kimberly Morales.
Main body text set in Billy Infant.
Typeface provided by SparkyType.
The illustrations in this book were created in mixed media (collage, pastels, colored pencils, gouache, and digital montage).

Library of Congress Cataloging-in-Publication Data

Names: Zeiger, Danna, author. | Bisaillon, Josée, illustrator.
Title: Rewriting the rules : how Dr. Kathleen Friel created new possibilities for brain research and disability / Danna Zeiger ; illustrated by Josée Bisaillon.
Description: Minneapolis : Millbrook Press, [2025] | Includes bibliographical references. | Audience: Ages 6–10. | Audience: Grades 2–3. | Summary: "As someone with cerebral palsy who runs a lab to help others with cerebral palsy, Dr. Kathleen Friel is rewriting the rules, defying expectations, and opening up new possibilities for herself and others"— Provided by publisher.
Identifiers: LCCN 2024054217 (print) | LCCN 2024054218 (ebook) | ISBN 9798765647271 (library binding) | ISBN 9798765682579 (epub)
Subjects: LCSH: Friel, Kathleen—Juvenile literature. | People with cerebral palsy—Biography—Juvenile literature. | Neurologists—Biography—Juvenile literature. | Physicians—Biography—Juvenile literature. | Medical research personnel—Biography—Juvenile literature. | Cerebral palsy—Juvenile literature.
Classification: LCC RC339.52.F83 Z45 2025 (print) | LCC RC339.52.F83 (ebook) | DDC 610.92 [B]—dc23/eng/20241202

LC record available at https://lccn.loc.gov/2024054217
LC ebook record available at https://lccn.loc.gov/2024054218

Manufactured in Guang Dong, China by Dream Colour Printing
1-1012028-53157-1/24/2025

REWRITING the RULES

How Dr. Kathleen Friel Created New Possibilities for Brain Research and Disability

Danna Zeiger
illustrated by **Josée Bisaillon**

Millbrook Press / Minneapolis

Dandelion wisps dared Kathleen to make wishes.
Kathleen blew.
Or, at least, she tried.

Kathleen's eyes blinked.
Her head shook.
Her arm trembled.
The fluffy seeds stayed stuck.

Kathleen was born with cerebral palsy,
and her muscles didn't always listen.

Instead of blowing, she fiercely flapped the flower.
At last, seeds sailed and laughter soared toward the sky.

When Kathleen was a toddler, her parents wanted to know how to help her learn to walk, to speak, and to do other things for herself.

They brought her to a doctor who told them the part of Kathleen's brain that controls her muscles had been injured when she was born. He said:

She will never walk normally.

She will never speak clearly.

She will never get better.

Send Kathleen to live in a place where others can take care of her so you can focus on your younger children.

NO WAY. Kathleen and her parents walked out the door, leaving behind that doctor forever.

They found a new doctor. He never wore socks but always wore a smile.
He told Kathleen's parents to treat her like any other child.

YES! That's exactly what they did.

They waited for her to put on her own shoes, even though it took her longer.

They expected her to complete her chores and clean up her toys.

And when she didn't, she got in trouble, just like her younger brothers did.

Kathleen had surgeries to help her walk.

But sometimes her muscles still tensed without warning.

She had speech therapy to help her form words.

But sentences still got stuck.

She had occupational therapy to help with everyday activities.

Even so, her body strained with every step.

Kathleen may have had to work harder in day-to-day life than other kids, but hard work was her normal.

Kathleen taught herself to do everything . . .
her own way.

How to fasten buttons.

How to cut up food.

And when she couldn't grasp her
favorite cereal . . .

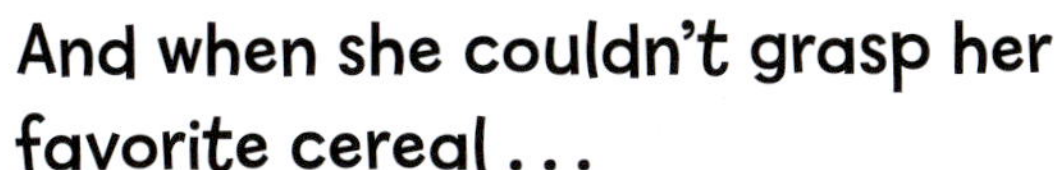

she licked her finger and dipped it in.

She rewrote the rules for even the
smallest movements.

At school, some kids made fun of her walk.

Ignored her questions.

Never picked her as a partner.

With the help of her parents, Kathleen explained why she moved differently,

how she was working on her speaking skills,

that her thoughts inside were crystal clear,
even if other kids didn't always understand her.

Soon, Kathleen's classmates realized that she liked

to play,

to giggle,

to imagine.

Speech therapy helped her get better at communicating, and her classmates got better at listening.

Kathleen had so much to offer the world, and she knew it.

In high school, science became Kathleen's favorite subject. Her teachers showed her that scientists found new solutions to problems, and she knew she wanted to do the same.

After all, she'd always been rewriting the rules.

In college, she learned that the brain is made of billions of connected cells. Some conditions, like cerebral palsy, can make those connections break down.

Most scientists thought that people with brain injuries like Kathleen's could not repair those broken connections.

But Kathleen wondered, What if an injured brain could make *new* connections?

What if she could rewrite the rules for treatment?

After college, Kathleen studied monkeys with brain injuries, hoping to discover ways to reshape their brain-cell connections. If she could find something that worked for monkeys, it might help people too. She tried training the monkeys to use the injured parts of their brains.

Typing on a computer was slow for Kathleen.
She experienced sudden muscle spasms,
strained eyes,
and exhaustion day after day
as she combed through months of monkey research videos.
She recorded observations, analyzed results, and wrote conclusions.
Until finally . . .

She held her breath as she finished her final graph.

Kathleen's experiments showed that training the monkeys created new brain connections.

She'd done it!

There was hope for recovery after all!

She had made an unsolvable problem . . . solvable.

After seven years of studying monkeys, Kathleen drew a shaky breath . . .

and carefully presented every word of her research to leading professors and brain experts.

Applause thundered.

Kathleen officially became Dr. Friel. She received her PhD, the highest educational degree possible. As an expert, Kathleen could now conduct her own experiments.

Once again, Kathleen had rewritten the rules for what she could achieve.

Kathleen started studying brain science at a new lab, and the first weeks there were uncomfortable.

Most people stared.

A few were silent.

Some were friendly.

She was the first scientist with cerebral palsy they'd met.

As the scientists got to know Kathleen,
they stopped staring and started listening.
Kathleen laughed loudly at jokes,
contributed to complicated science discussions,
and wore Patriots and Red Sox gear in her New York lab
at every opportunity.

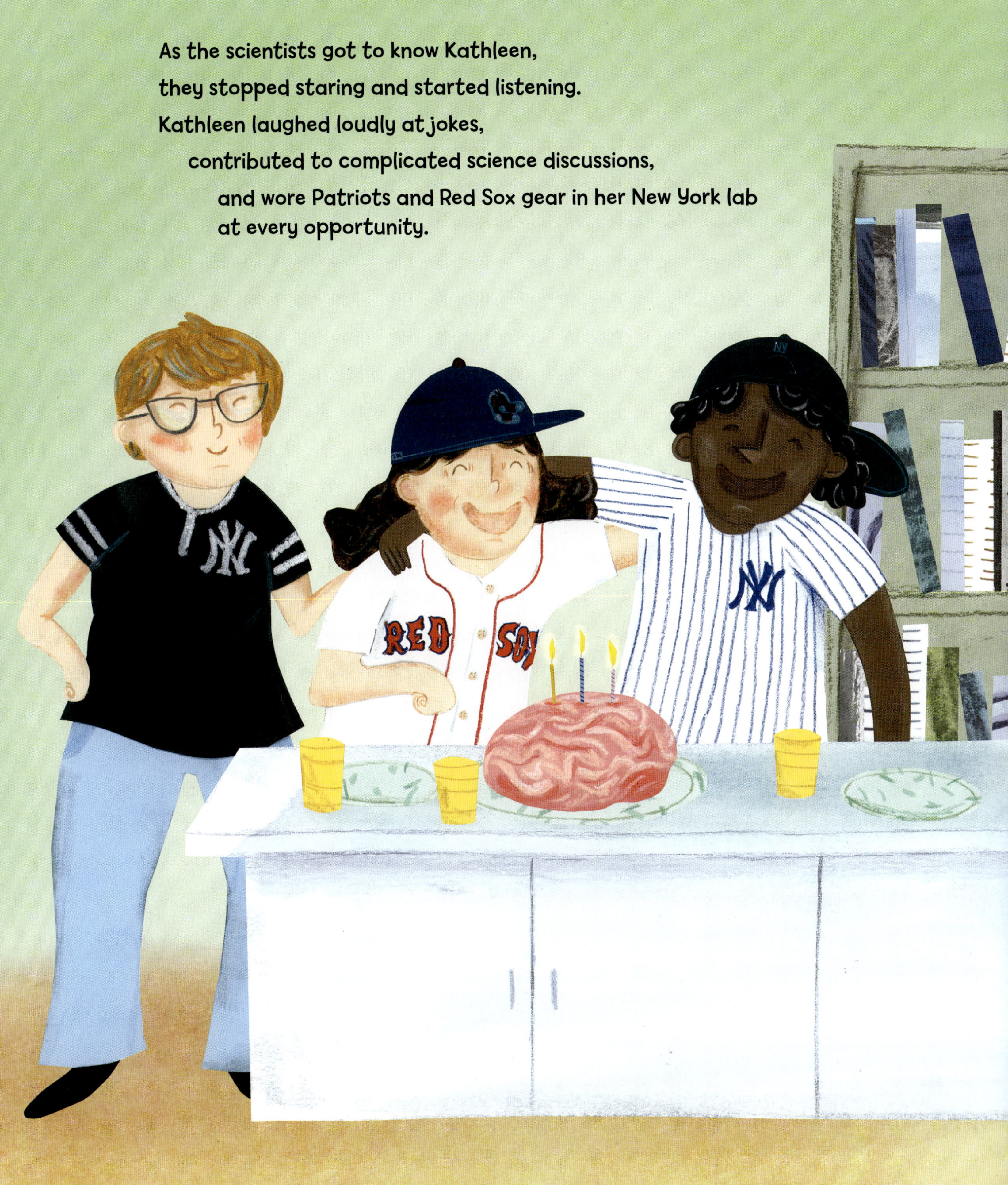

Outside the lab, Kathleen struggled with strangers who didn't know how to treat someone who moved and talked differently.

Sometimes, people would grab her, thinking they were helping to keep her from falling—only to hurt her.

A cashier at a fast-food restaurant didn't believe she could order or pay for her own food. She left hungry and got food elsewhere.

And some doctors treated her as if she couldn't understand information about her own body, despite being a well-known scientist!

Over and over, Kathleen explained that she could make her own decisions. She was in charge. Kathleen needed to advocate for herself so others would listen. This was exhausting, but when they finally understood, it made a difference.

At work, Kathleen was ready to use the tools she'd developed for animals to help kids with cerebral palsy. She created her own research lab where she continues to rewrite the rules for people with disabilities.

Today, Kathleen welcomes people with cerebral palsy to participate in experiments. She conducts tests to see which treatments help best.

Kathleen has cerebral palsy, and she rock climbs,

she bikes,

and she skis.

And after nine years of punches, kicks, and board-breaking, she earned a black belt in Taekwondo.

In Kathleen's lab, children with cerebral palsy learn to write their own rules using therapies she developed.

These kids like Kathleen because she's funny, she leads her own science lab, and she has cerebral palsy, like them.

After weeks of intensive camp and coaching, the kids' hand function improves.

Their muscles strengthen.

New brain connections form.

They have special pictures taken of their brain and wear special headbands that help measure changes in brain connections.

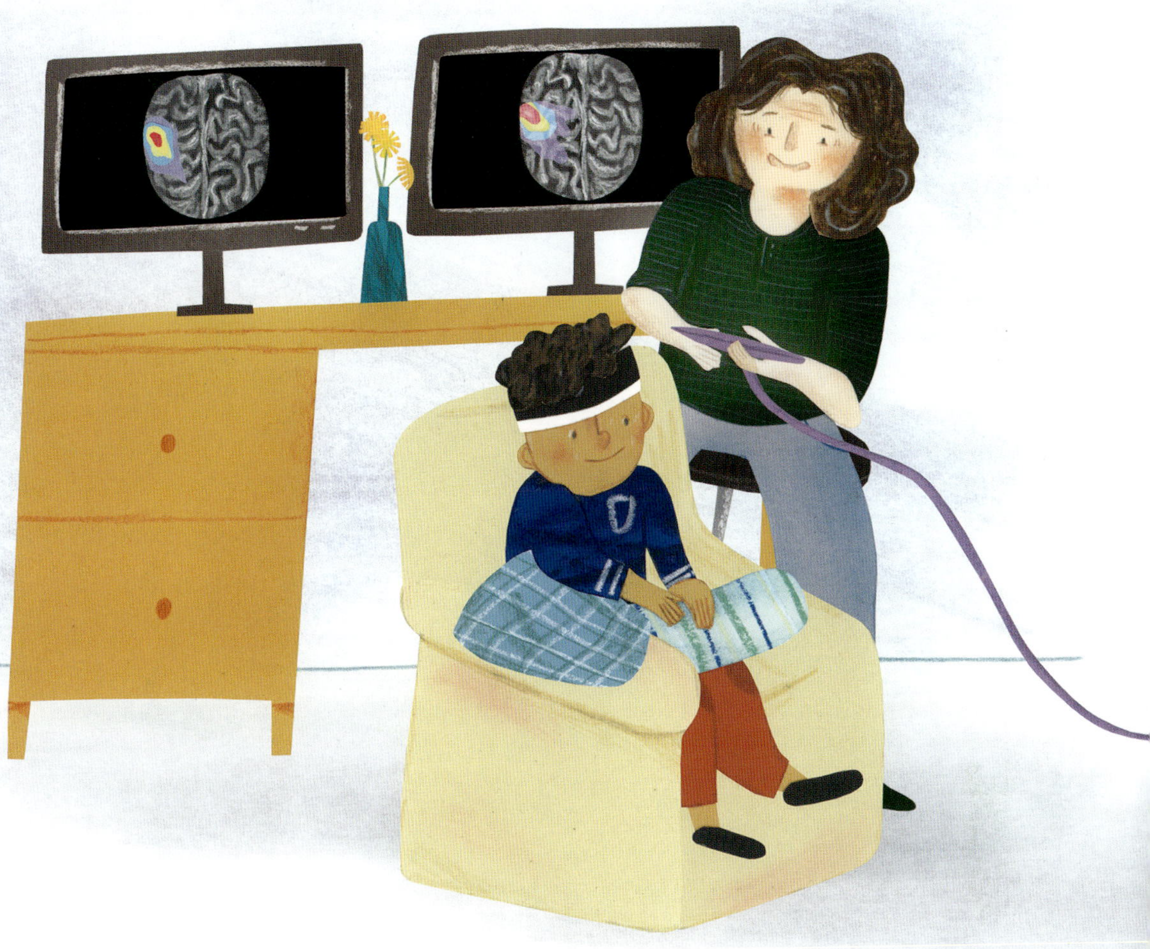

One day they too may climb rocks or break boards or run research labs.

The world is full of limitations,
but as Kathleen discovered,
there are many ways to wish on dandelion wisps.
Kathleen just had to find her own.

Kathleen and her research are paving the way for people with cerebral palsy and other disabilities
to be heard,
to find their own approaches,
and to rewrite the rules.

AUTHOR'S NOTE

I was a college student when I first met Kathleen. I had joined a new research lab where smart, intimidating people conducted brain research. Kathleen, an established scientist, was assigned to be my mentor.

Kathleen was not the only person I knew with cerebral palsy (CP). However, I had never met someone with CP in the sciences. Kathleen's tenacity, scientific rigor, and intellect—not to mention her kindness, patience, and gentle guidance—made a strong impression on everyone in the lab.

Through Kathleen, I have also witnessed society's stereotypes, hurtful assumptions, and coldhearted exclusion of people with disabilities. Mistreatment, mean comments, and constant dismissiveness of one of the smartest people I know—and a distinguished scientist—have horrified me. Observing these failures to accommodate her (and others) after she already persevered and succeeded in a challenging male-dominated STEM field has rudely awakened me to the many uninclusive aspects of daily life.

In addition to having cerebral palsy, Kathleen was diagnosed with breast cancer in 2018 and has continued running her lab while going through treatments. Unfortunately, people with CP are statistically more likely to develop chronic diseases, such as cancer. The events in this book take place before her diagnosis, which is why she is depicted in the art with longer hair. Kathleen says, "I don't think of myself accomplishing much *despite* my health. Instead, I've been able to accomplish some things *because of* my health adventures."

Kathleen has taught me a lot of complicated scientific concepts and techniques over the years. However, the most valuable lesson she taught me, which I hope readers glean from this book, is this: People who think or move differently "have so much to offer!" As Kathleen explains, "Don't dismiss us or view us as burdens or liabilities. Listen to us, engage with us as equals. We will do the same for you." She adds, "People with CP—and other disabilities—want to be known as people. We have rich social lives, hobbies, favorite sports teams. . . . We're more than the way we move or talk."

Let's take notes from the great strides and impact Kathleen has made, and let's rewrite the rules.

The author and Kathleen Friel in 2024

MORE ABOUT KATHLEEN, HER RESEARCH, AND HER ADVOCACY

Scientists used to think that brain injuries caused permanent losses of abilities. If connections in a brain were broken, they assumed the functions controlled by the injured brain regions were gone forever.

At the same time, scientists knew that healthy brains could make new connections. For example, typing on a computer or playing the piano every day strengthens the part of the brain that controls finger movements. Kathleen asked, What if an injured brain could make new connections too? What if the healthy part could compensate and help someone regain lost use?

She started by testing treatment ideas in animals. Each monkey in the lab had an injured side of the brain and a healthy side of the brain. Fingers connected to the injured side didn't work as well.

Kathleen showed that if monkeys practiced a skill—such as grabbing food—using fingers controlled by an injured side of the brain, they could improve their brain connections.

Building on her monkey research, Kathleen and her colleagues tested cats with brain injuries mimicking cerebral palsy. Training cats to use paws connected to the injured parts of their brains helped them form new brain connections. The uninjured healthy areas of the brain took over so that some function came back.

If this sort of training worked for animals, Kathleen thought maybe it could work for kids too. And her research has shown that it does. Kids with CP can build bridges in their brains around their injuries. With focused hand therapy, they can strengthen muscles, brain, and spinal cord connections.

As a director of the Clinical Laboratory for Early Brain Injury Recovery at the Burke Neurological Institute in White Plains, New York, Kathleen—along with her colleagues—evaluates exactly which connections are injured in the brains of kids with CP. At this institute, kids can also participate in research focused on new treatments to help them. Before Kathleen and her colleagues created this program, very few treatment centers existed for restoring function in kids with brain injuries.

Kathleen Friel

Kathleen has received many prestigious awards for her research and disability advocacy, including the 2017 Corbett Ryan Pathways Pioneer Award by the American Academy for Cerebral Palsy and Developmental Medicine, the 2021 National Cerebral Palsy Awareness Research Award, the 2022 Cerebral Palsy Foundation Healthcare Visionary Leadership Award, and the 2023 American Academy for Cerebral Palsy and Developmental Medicine Mentorship Award.

Kathleen has shown that experience leads to changes in the brain. Similarly, she feels that "experience drives changes in society. So we are the ones who drive change." She continues to be a strong advocate for those with CP, focusing on abilities—not impairments—as well as accessibility and respect.

MORE ABOUT CEREBRAL PALSY

Cerebral palsy is the most common motor (movement) disability in childhood. As Kathleen writes, "Approximately 3 in 1,000 people have CP, which translates to approximately 800,000 people in the United States, and over 18 million people worldwide. . . . To put these numbers in perspective, 800,000 people is equivalent to the population of Seattle, and 18 million individuals is equivalent to the population of the state of New York."

CP happens when a child's brain gets injured. This can happen either before a child is born, during birth, or soon after birth. There are many possible reasons for brain injury in early childhood, including childbirth itself, car accidents, and even infections. Depending on the type of injury, how severe it is, when it occurs during a child's development, and where exactly in the brain it is, it can have a wide range of impacts.

People are affected by CP in different ways because their disability depends upon which areas of their brain are injured. CP always impacts movement. Sometimes, CP can also affect a person's ability to see, hear, talk, or think.

For more information about CP or to find ways to support research efforts, please visit the Cerebral Palsy Foundation's website at yourcpf.org.

MORE ABOUT THE BRAIN

The brain controls how we think, remember, feel, and move. It handles things we usually don't even notice, such as our breathing, our heartbeat, and our body temperature. Different parts of the brain are responsible for different aspects of our body, like hearing, seeing, smelling, or remembering.

Cerebral palsy often affects the primary motor cortex—the strip of the brain that controls our muscles. Different sections along this strip are in charge of making specific muscles move.

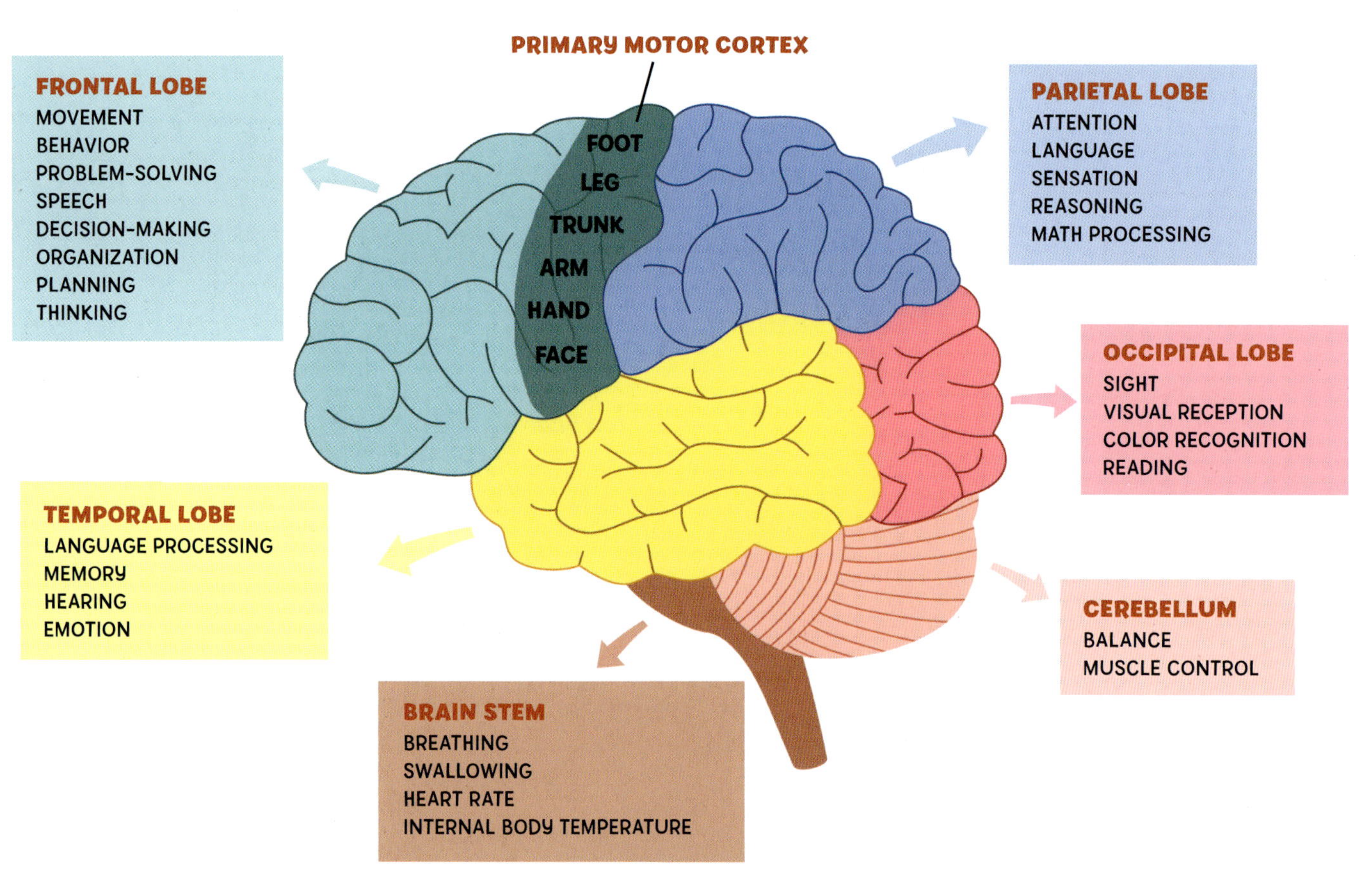

QUOTATION SOURCES

"I don't think of . . . my health adventures": "Unstoppable: How Dr. Kathleen Friel Has Made Incredible Accomplishments Despite Cerebral Palsy and Metastatic Breast Cancer," *Authority Magazine*. Medium, July 10, 2020, https://medium.com/authority-magazine/unstoppable-how-dr-kathleen-friel-has-made-incredible-accomplishments-despite-cerebral-palsy-and-m-f69860fec6d5.

"have so much to offer": "Dr Friel Receives the 2017 Corbett Ryan Pathways Pioneer Award (Clip)," YouTube video, 1:17, posted by Burke Neurological Institute, November 13, 2017, https://www.youtube.com/watch?v=xAiamcEPVQ8.

"Don't dismiss us . . . same for you": "Unstoppable," *Authority Magazine*.

"People with CP . . . we move or talk": "Let's Change the Future of Cerebral Palsy!," Burke Neurological Institute, March 1, 2021, https://burke.weill.cornell.edu/friel-lab/impact/news-articles/let%E2%80%99s-change-future-cerebral-palsy.

"experience drives changes . . . who drive change": "Dr Friel," YouTube video.

"Approximately 3 in 1,000 . . . state of New York": Kathleen M. Friel, "Cerebral Palsy and Breast Cancer," Surviving Breast Cancer, August 7, 2022, https://www.survivingbreastcancer.org/post/cerebral-palsy-and-breast-cancer.

SELECTED BIBLIOGRAPHY

Friel, Kathleen M. "Cerebral Palsy and Breast Cancer." Surviving Breast Cancer, August 7, 2022. http://www.survivingbreastcancer.org/post/cerebral-palsy-and-breast-cancer.

Friel, Kathleen M., Archie A. Heddings, and Randolph J. Nudo. "Effects of Postlesion Experience on Behavioral Recovery and Neurophysiologic Reorganization After Cortical Injury in Primates." *Neurorehabilitation & Neural Repair* 14, no. 3 (February 2000): 187–198.

"Scientist Demonstrates Personal Triumph over Cerebral Palsy as She Treats Children with Brain Injuries at Burke Medical Research Institute." Yahoo Finance, July 30, 2013. https://finance.yahoo.com/news/scientist-demonstrates-personal-triumph-over-190843380.html.

"Spotlight Interview with Dr. Kathleen M. Friel." Burke Neurological Institute, October 4, 2019. http://burke.weill.cornell.edu/friel-lab/impact/news-articles/spotlight-interview-dr-kathleen-m-friel.

"Unstoppable: How Dr. Kathleen Friel Has Made Incredible Accomplishments Despite Cerebral Palsy and Metastatic Breast Cancer." *Authority Magazine*, Medium, July 10, 2020. http://medium.com/authority-magazine/unstoppable-how-dr-kathleen-friel-has-made-incredible-accomplishments-despite-cerebral-palsy-and-m-f69860fec6d5.

A complete list of sources is available on the author's website. https://www.dannazeiger.com

FIND OUT MORE

To learn more about Kathleen's lab research, visit the Friel Lab's YouTube Channel: https://www.youtube.com/@friellab1668

Read more about the brain, for picture book readers: McAnulty, Stacy. *Brains! Not Just a Zombie Snack*. New York: Godwin Books, 2021.

Read more about the brain, for middle grade readers: Woollcott, Tory. *The Brain: The Ultimate Thinking Machine*. New York: First Second, 2018.

Read more about the brain, for older readers: Farinella, Matteo, and Hana Roš. *Neurocomic*. London: Nobrow, 2014.